Ferryboats

Martina Thomson

23.5.10   Terriano Muting House

to Rachel

with love,

Martina.

Hearing Eye

HEARING EYE
TORRIANO MEETING HOUSE
POETRY PAMPHLET SERIES No. 54

Hearing Eye
Box 1, 99 Torriano Avenue
London NW5 2RX, UK
email: hearing_eye@torriano.org
www.torriano.org

ISBN: 9781905082360

Warm thanks to Jane Duran, Susan Johns and Mimi Khalvati.

Cover: Ceramic ferryboat and photograph by Martina Thomson, design by
Hannah Turin.

This publication has been made possible with
the financial support of Arts Council England

Printed by Catford Print Centre

Contents

Glaze Test 5

Morandi's Still Life 6

David 7

If I lie still 8

Blondes 9

A Story 10

Witness 11

Silver Spoon 12

Tristanstrasse 13

My Mother's Ferry 14

Sundays 15

Swoop of the Eagle 16

Rose-Red 17

Frau Trümpler 18

Anna's Garden 19

Isle of Sylt 20

New Snow on the Mountain 21

The Bookbinder 22

Zucker und Zimt 23

Night-watch 24

Noah in the Vineyard 25

Nello in Railton Road 26

Elegy for CLR 27

My Friend in France 28

Wing-beats 29

The Letter 30

Sponge Fossil 31

From a Dream-book 32

It is the Hour 32

Glaze Test

The contours of three brushstrokes
on my test piece are edged

in orange by iron oxide
which glaze and flame

have wakened in the clay,
fine, wavering lines

as if traced in pencil
by Morandi. And so

the line a hill draws
in the sky has thrilled me,

ever-shifting versions
as I walk towards it –

so many goes at touch
and demarcation.

Morandi's Still-life

Three bottles and a jug,
two dark square jars –
their edges waver,
one becomes the other,
interlaced they are embedded
in the background and the ground
on which they stand.
Or look again and see
two upright planes
on which assembled shapes are go-betweens;
motes of dust detach themselves
from contours and venture out
on tender explorations.
Bottles, jug and jars have dematerialised,
are sentient
and forever shift.
I think of rooms that held
such play – of look, or touch
or mere proximity –
but now are barren.

David

Your chair I can touch now, it doesn't attack me,
your coat still hangs there but has no power.
All around here what there was is expended.
You don't disturb me. Perhaps I'm forgetting you.

But there's no safety on the roads beyond Galway
where snipers linger at crossroads – signposts
with names barely familiar target my chest.
Spiddal, Oughterard, Carraroe and Carna.

Sleepwalker, I'm drawn to the pub by the pier,
the one with the fish-shed askew beside it,
and on entering know we sat here –
I take the black drink of your absence.

If I lie still

I am as the dry sand high on the beach
moulded by footprints
with stone, glass and shells,
driftwood and rope
my random acquisitions.
The slight distinct imprint of plovers' feet
might almost rouse me;
storms and high winds have no power.
This flat stretch is forever.

See the pink petals of my tulips
wide open, too wide,
the lightest pink and white,
the petal on the table
shell-like, asking for nothing,
holding no treasure.

Blondes

Mists hold the meadow, no sun,
the grassy path sodden, black.
And the long swathes of dried grass
on the ground beside it have gone,
those swathes of blond hair
that made me feel so tender.

Only yesterday I knelt
to touch, to stroke them,
knowing how you wouldn't have
resisted such appeal.

A Story

He brought her back to make her his wife.
She did not consent but liked the adventure.

He folded her to him, held her close.
She felt she could swim in his summer smell.

He held out a towel for her after her bath.
She preferred to dive to the warmth of his body.

His eyes followed a baitish girl.
Hers fell to the ground with him up to his tricks.

He corrected her English, taught her the conditional.
'But I'd know how to use it, should I want to use it.'

His handwriting was clear, performed elegant loops.
Hers full of gaps barely touched the page.

His pages made books, his books filled shelves.
She moulded clay, played with the river.

He saw her, a seal, swim out to the sea.
She saw him, a hare, leap up to the moon.

Witness

The old Pither stove,
a black iron column,
now bears a dish
which offers onions,
bulbs of garlic, laurel leaves.
There was a daily ritual,
the tending of the stove:
the setting of the draught
the riddling down of ashes
the fetching up of coal
the raising of the lid
the rain of coal released –
the rubbly sound of coal
through years of winter months.

Silver Spoon

The small silver spoon
in the palm of my hand
my fingers across it
my thumb in its hollow –

The silver tarnished
the slim stem buckled
I like the feel of it
don't want to let go.

Small yellow coffee cups
set out on a tray
with a spoon in each saucer –
dazzling sugar-lumps
and a bowl of whipped cream.

Staged in the blue room
among her friends
I hear my mother ask
'Ein Mokka?'

That scene can't be played again
the set was struck
the players condemned.

This sliver of a spoon
slipped through, and here
I have it in my hand.

Tristanstrasse

The milk-cart rattles over cobblestones,
the high, clear sound of Hübner's bell,
froth to the brim in the jug they hold,
rides can be cadged, the pony stroked.

Then milk-vans come on rubber tyres,
'hurry up, quick,' a hooter calling,
blunt bottles handed over coldly –
still it is summer and she loves her frocks.

But listen, black boots now click in the street,
a staccato flagsong disrupts the day.
The dog is poisoned, lies yelping and dies
while their father keeps vigil stretched on the sofa.

From her desk at school she sees a man fall
across the window: a pause in the classroom.
'A shop's been burgled, the church is on fire!'
'Ah, you don't know', says the piano teacher.

Suddenly packers are in their house:
she runs to the garden to bury her dolls.
Thomas goes away to an English school,
when winter comes she too is sent.

Their room in London is in that street
where the buildings all look exactly the same.
Her tongue dances a new language in her mouth
and she makes a secret of her childhood words.

My Mother's Ferry

The attic's the place where my mother stays young –
bob-haired, slim – she leads the dance.
Mothballs bounce, roll on the boards
as she lifts woolly vests from iron trunks.

The ceiling's pitched, the rafters hold
a porthole washed by stars and moon,
we're launched in the hull of a sky-bound boat –
our cargo of hat-boxes artfully stacked,
the tailor's dummy at the helm.

Flotsam, attic-drawn souls climb aboard,
jump their stories, bum in for the trip;
Dorian Gray has hung his portrait up,
peers closely at the leer it gains,
contrives to paint his beauty back.

The girl who must spin her straw into gold
fingers the rustling fabric in tears –
light work for Rumpelstiltskin who slips in at night,
then rips himself up in a temper tantrum;
bits of him lie about in corners.

Uncle Kulka, who I know put his head in the oven,
now hums his tune and comes to join us
when my mother rummages in fancy-dress gear
and we fan ourselves with ostrich feathers.

Sundays

On Sunday mornings the bathroom was the place to be,
here, to see my mother and my aunt
dance round each other in the steam
as they stepped into the bath to take their shower,
their nakedness up close. My mother's breasts
were apples, she was fair, the water silvered her,
my aunt was olive skinned, her breasts were long
and hung like pears as from a wind-blown branch.

Her arm outstretched had darkness at its root,
between her legs the dark shape that I looked for
and only here on Sundays dark hair fell about her –
I'd spin out time and brush my teeth forever.
Their words came out too loud or muffled by the drains;
then the towelling chapter, the good smell from the powder
which puffed them from the room in shapeless gowns.

Soon after them my father took his bath.
I've seen him lie there long, his head made pink,
offered on a rubber pillow, and half-way down his length
the flannel he kept floating in just that position
and never shifted even though I asked.
But he was easy in the bathroom, sang
his Russian song and teased me and I liked it.

When guests arrived for coffee, cake, the endless talk
and ping-pong in the garden, my family made me shy –
to have them glisten so, the way they leant back
in their chairs, pursed their lips or twisted, stretched
to take a light, the way they threw their laughter out
like questions – were they given to water still?
The morning steam gleamed and hung.

Swoop of the Eagle

The magician is back, the whistle in the garden
and already his boomerang is high,
spinning above the scraggy pines,

returning obedient to his command
and again and again he sends it away –
still the two beside him skip for more.

Till a flame leaps out of his beak-like mouth,
flutters with menace about them both;
the orange silk square he ties round her wrist,

pulls clean and painlessly through her bone,
draws as a worm out of her ear.
The children ask for a glimpse of the gaps

which he's cut in his jacket for air to the armpits
for 'man needs air just like a bird'.
With his arms outstretched he soars like an eagle.

Enlacing his fingers, his arms now pendulous,
he makes them a swing for rides in turn,
she and her friend in their summer frocks.

When he puts her down she is thoughtful,
looks at her friend and is thoughtful,
shakes her head to a second go.

Rose-Red

He was leaning against the garden wall of the
Humperdincks' where the gate was always locked, the
garden itself overgrown, so wild that you couldn't see the
house but you could guess at it. Mr. Humperdinck was
famous, he had written operas and I knew about his dark
blue, starlit bath. Further back, not far from Mother
Holle's well, stood Rose-Red's cottage where on winter
nights she let the bear come in to warm up by the fire. The
grey man held his frozen fingers up, rose-red sausages of
Plasticine, asked me to help him with his buttons. They
were easy buttons but then, suddenly, I ran away. I left
him standing at the Humperdincks' and my mittens on the
pavement.

Frau Trümpler

The sewing machine was set up by the window in the Kinderzimmer. When we heard it was Frau Trümpler's day, we thumped up the stairs, then paused at the door, entered shyly because we knew we'd look – first thing – to see whether her two 'angels' sat in place on the windowsill. And there they were, two dumpy white paper bags, each with two ears, two wings twisted up. She was round and dumpy herself and smiled and never forgot. She lived above the sweet-shop. The wicker basket was stacked with her things: sheets and towels to patch, my father's collars to turn, Tom's torn pockets, the hems of my frocks. I liked to settle by her on the floor and journey along, her knee making the engine buzz – start-stop, run-stop – and when a sheet came down and folded me in, I travelled in her boat, picked out a raspberry sweet. Two passengers stood beside me, Frau Trümpler's feet in plum lisle stockings and blunt shoes – strangers.

Anna's Garden

The lion, the ram and the sheep walk about in Anna's garden. The lion and the ram walk proudly with their heads held high. The spotted wolf is hungry open-mouthed and hunched. There are no people to sit on the ornate seats under the vine-covered trellis, the girl in the long white dress plays her lute and waits. She's two-dimensional like the other figures, painted on both sides and on her own lead stand. The gardener is headless but carries a watering-can that spouts a silver arc. A man kneels naked on a pedestal as if under a spell. I place the red-billed stork beside the palm tree with red fruit. The rose bush is in bloom, the monkey offers a coconut – no one takes it, it's held in the air.

Isle of Sylt

Homme libre, toujours tu chériras la mer...Charles Baudelaire

Anna, do you remember when you took me
to that North Sea island,
my one wish was to see the night,
be out and awake under the night sky,
walk by the sea,
not mind rain if it came.

You said we might do it in halves,
walk a half-night, then sleep
and the next day you'd wake me at midnight
for us to set out.

And I woke with you bending over me,
how clumsy I was with my clothes,
how we stole to the door like burglars,
ran free from the house
down to the sea which was loud.

Our walk to the tip of the island,
how we stood at an outpost in blackness
with waves crashing in on two sides.
Homme libre, toujours tu chériras la mer.

Your lopsided friend taught me those words,
stomping among bathers, hand in the air;
he'd embarrassed me with his urgent
declamation, bare pasty body, his limp.
His name was Peschkowsky –
did he survive?

Later I learned the whole poem –
the bitterness it contains.

New Snow on the Mountain

Anna was lying on the couch
by the window, the remains of a dream.
In words I bent down to she told me
she'd brought the oleander in,
where I would find the folder
with the letters and how I must carry her
to some altar place when she was dead.
Her death was the slightest shift.

I lifted her body, which was light,
resting on my arms like a casket
structured of moth-wings –
white, grey and violet.

The Bookbinder

The name Van Gogh in large green capitals
on fawn, cut from the book my mother has re-bound,
is pasted on the cover. She took grey linen
for the binding and I see her struggle to make good –
the way the endpapers are strained to line
the inside of the boards. I like this imperfection,
hear her breathing as she glues and sews together
pages that had fallen apart – shoulders bent,
the right always ahead, as in her crab-like walk
when suddenly she flipped down to pick a bit of green
or fallen blossom from the pavement, held
between her fingers like an offering till she found
a hedge, a patch of earth or grass to vouchsafe
a softer death – so obstinate in her care.

Zucker und Zimt

For my grandmother

She held it in her hands as a potter holds clay,
the warm yeast dough for Apfelstrudel,
dumped it on the damask she'd spread on the table,
began to knead in a rock-a-bye motion.
Small nibbles were allowed from the raisins in the bowl,
the pared, sliced apples, the *Zucker und Zimt.*

And now with the rolling-pin the work of a master:
she began from the middle, pushed out her fabric
always from the middle, like a tide it reached further
a domain expanding with soft, scalloped edges
growing pearly, precious, a baby skin, see-through
it annexed and possessed the entire stretch –
hands to her back in relief when she'd done,
her smile and her nod for me to begin.

At once all fingers into the apples,
fistfuls to be dropped on to the dough-cloth
evenly, evenly, and again and again, then I rained
down the raisins, seed-scattered the bread-crumbs
and from the height of my silver spoon cruising
bestowed the valediction, the *Zucker und Zimt.*

A *pas-de-deux* followed, one each side of the table
we lifted the damask, unsaddled the dough-cloth,
in measured pavane we nudged the thing forward
so it rolled and enfolded its bulky harvest.
Step by step the roll expanded till its stuffed belly
slumped. My grandmother made it a crescent moon.

Night-watch

My grandmother unwrapped her legs as she sat,
a snow mountain, on my mother's bed.

I watched her in pretended sleep
from the mattress I camped on for her visit.

Over and under she unwound the bandage
from above her knee down to her ankle,

round and about, a fairy-tale task,
the roll growing clumsy in her hands.

They were boneless legs all softness and
goodness, seal-pups pitted like porridge

which she folded away into the bolsters.
The bedsprings sang as they received her.

When the light was out, I heard her prayer.

Noah in the Vineyard

When Noah touched the earth, laid his face
against it and in tears, disbelieving,
thanked his God for the great gift –

when the animals trotted to pasture in twos,
and the boys wrestled, romped, testing the ground –
when a girl, so shy, danced while the wives
with babies, with bundles, gathered in reverence –
there were two left in the ark who rebelled,
a boy and his favourite sister.

They'd loved the face of the water too much
and now returned their craft to the ebbing flood
that drew them down from Ararat,
bore them over drowned Saharas,
conceded them to oceans where
wave and whirlwind cast them astray.
The legend leads to many endings

and Father Noah, God's good man,
who tills his plot, stakes his vineyard,
still walks on sea-legs, sorrows for seascapes
and, under the moon, lies naked and drunk.

Nello in Railton Road

An upstairs corner room, not large – two windows
make it light – his bed along one side
and on the other are the shelves built up on bricks
that hold his books; across one corner stands the desk,
full of matter, where his secretary works
and opposite: his chair, close to the television.
The ship from outpost stations anchored here.

Two flat palms rubbed together flip off
in different directions, balletic mime that says:
I've done with it. He takes his Shakespeare from the shelf,
but keeps an eye too on the screen. When he stands up
I see that half his height is gone, so folded
forward is he from the middle; still slim and elegant.

The bustle in the office down below deals with the world.
We are alone and he is glad, 'No need for me
now to "arrange" myself ', and like a private thought
hums notes of Palestrina. He wants a fish.
'One with a head and tail', two fingers show the length.
And so I find one in the market and we celebrate.

'From 3 to 6 to 9, that childhood time I think of,
I was bright, I now think I was bright,
in Tunapuna, and my mother – God, she read.'
He will not leave his haven yet has schemes:
'Florence, any time, the hills above the town.
If someone took me by the ears I'd go tomorrow'.
Would he though? He sits it out.
His patience is the treasure in the room.

Elegy for C.L.R.

His fingers are like
        the strings of an instrument,
when he raises them
        the air makes music.
His words are agile creatures
        that ferret out distinctions,
his thoughts pliant girders
        that span distances.
A figure dark and erect –
        slouchy hat, bundle of books.

My Friend in France

i.m. Philip O'Connor

Elegant in his white suit,
lately bearded, he giggles a lot –
nose and lips twitch, rabbit-like,
ready to sniff out some little falsity.
Of the dainty dishes he prepares
he eats barely a mouthful,
dives instead into cupboards
to make sure the stock of wine
won't fail him. And talks and splutters,
eyes wide open, startled by his own words.

Reversal and attack are his tactics.
'You lack ugliness' he says, and repeats,
fond of his phrase. His irreverences
have my children in stitches.
He likes them on his side.

His Journal is his 'free-flow'
morning ablution – single typed pages,
never re-read or corrected,
laid one on top of another,
grown over the years to a column.
They are shelved now
in an archive in the States.

After his death I slept in his room
with his books and gramophone
and the clothes I knew on the rail.
His cat came in and out during the night.
I took his soft grey scarf the morning I left.

Wing-beats

The lightest flutter,
he threw it over my head, lassoed me,
drew me to him and smiled –
a white shawl of flimsy stuff.

In the plane I clenched it in my hand,
my head pressed hard against the window-pane
above the snow-draped mountains of Iran –
clear, every fold, a puckered shawl laid out.

His gift is stowed now in a wooden box
painted with tigers and blue peaks
and, on the inside of the lid, white birds
stretched between sky and sea.

The Letter

Now, after some weeks
the longing for a letter
builds up in me.

It's a sparse garden we keep
with few plants growing
and where between here
and your distant land
must I imagine it?

Is it like that patch you pointed to
across our stream, on the icy slope,
a garden remote, staked out in wilderness,
its neat rows tended –
a sampler hanging in a field of snow?

A letter from you now
would shed such seeds of joy
I would spend days up there
digging, planting and watering.

Sponge Fossil

The stone you gave me on that winter beach
at Cuckmere Haven
lies on my kitchen table.
The fossil of a sponge, you said.

I like to hold it in my hands,
chalk, and chips of flint,
a wasps nest,
or point and rounded shoulders of a heart.
Much dashed about by stormy seas
its gashes here and there can make it grin
or form the thoughtful profile of a fish.

It's the hollow that I treasure,
the softness of the creature that once lived here
seen in the hard crust.

From a Dream-book

The car I drove and parked
was a heap of earth
when I looked back.
His desk too
was newly dug-up earth,
the shape of an awkward grand,
its wing stretched out.

I woke up sad
as if I'd lost my words
and it was coming to December.

It is the Hour

It is the hour when lovers' vows
Seem sweet...   Byron

It's light, but early yet,
I lie a while, then know
now is the time.

Why is it so good
to move in a house of sleepers,
to find the bolt, draw it back,

step out and walk away?
I walk across the morning grass.